This JOURNAL Belongs To:

_____

_____

_____

DATE:

Today's Message:
_____
_____

SCRIPTURE

SERMON Notes:

# How Does This Message Challenge Me?

_____
_____
_____
_____
_____
_____
_____

## HOW CAN I APPLY THE LESSON THIS WEEK?

## Prayer Requests

_____
_____
_____
_____
_____
_____
_____
_____
_____

## UPCOMING ACTIVITIES & REMINDERS

DATE:

Today's Message:
_____
_____

SCRIPTURE

SERMON Notes:

_____
_____
_____
_____
_____
_____
_____
_____
_____
_____
_____
_____
_____
_____
_____
_____
_____
_____
_____
_____
_____
_____
_____
_____
_____
_____
_____
_____
_____

# How Does This Message Challenge Me?

_____
_____
_____
_____
_____
_____
_____

## HOW CAN I APPLY THE LESSON THIS WEEK?




## Prayer Requests

_____
_____
_____
_____
_____
_____
_____
_____

## UPCOMING ACTIVITIES & REMINDERS

DATE:

Today's Message:

_____

_____

# SCRIPTURE

SERMON *Notes:*

# How Does This Message Challenge Me?

_____
_____
_____
_____
_____
_____

## HOW CAN I APPLY THE LESSON THIS WEEK?

## Prayer Requests

_____
_____
_____
_____
_____
_____
_____
_____

## UPCOMING ACTIVITIES& REMINDERS

DATE:

Today's Message:

_____

_____

SCRIPTURE ___

SERMON Notes:

_____
_____
_____
_____
_____
_____
_____
_____
_____
_____
_____
_____
_____
_____
_____
_____
_____
_____
_____
_____
_____
_____
_____
_____
_____
_____
_____

# How Does This Message Challenge Me?

_____
_____
_____
_____
_____
_____
_____

## HOW CAN I APPLY THE LESSON THIS WEEK?

## Prayer Requests

_____
_____
_____
_____
_____
_____
_____
_____

## UPCOMING ACTIVITIES & REMINDERS

DATE:

Today's Message:

_____

_____

SCRIPTURE

SERMON Notes:

# How Does This Message Challenge Me?

_____
_____
_____
_____
_____
_____

## HOW CAN I APPLY THE LESSON THIS WEEK?

## Prayer Requests

_____
_____
_____
_____
_____
_____
_____
_____

## UPCOMING ACTIVITIES & REMINDERS

DATE:

Today's Message:

_____

_____

SCRIPTURE

SERMON Notes:

_____
_____
_____
_____
_____
_____
_____
_____
_____
_____
_____
_____
_____
_____
_____
_____
_____
_____
_____
_____
_____
_____
_____
_____
_____
_____
_____
_____
_____

# How Does This Message Challenge Me?

_____
_____
_____
_____
_____
_____
_____

## HOW CAN I APPLY THE LESSON THIS WEEK?

## Prayer Requests

_____
_____
_____
_____
_____
_____
_____
_____
_____

## UPCOMING ACTIVITIES & REMINDERS

DATE:

## Today's Message:

_____

_____

# SCRIPTURE

## SERMON Notes:

# How Does This Message Challenge Me?

_____
_____
_____
_____
_____

## HOW CAN I APPLY THE LESSON THIS WEEK?




## Prayer Requests

_____
_____
_____
_____
_____
_____
_____

## UPCOMING ACTIVITIES & REMINDERS

DATE:

Today's Message:
_____
_____

SCRIPTURE _____

SERMON Notes:

# How Does This Message Challenge Me?

_____
_____
_____
_____
_____
_____
_____

## HOW CAN I APPLY THE LESSON THIS WEEK?




## Prayer Requests

_____
_____
_____
_____
_____
_____
_____
_____

## UPCOMING ACTIVITIES & REMINDERS

DATE:

Today's Message:

_____

_____

SCRIPTURE

SERMON Notes:

_____
_____
_____
_____
_____
_____
_____
_____
_____
_____
_____
_____
_____
_____
_____
_____
_____
_____
_____
_____
_____
_____
_____
_____
_____
_____
_____

# How Does This Message Challenge Me?

_____
_____
_____
_____
_____
_____
_____

## HOW CAN I APPLY THE LESSON THIS WEEK?




## Prayer Requests

_____
_____
_____
_____
_____
_____
_____
_____
_____

## UPCOMING ACTIVITIES & REMINDERS

DATE:

Today's Message:
_____

_____

SCRIPTURE

SERMON Notes:

# How Does This Message Challenge Me?

_____

_____

_____

_____

_____

_____

## HOW CAN I APPLY THE LESSON THIS WEEK?

## Prayer Requests

_____

_____

_____

_____

_____

_____

_____

_____

## UPCOMING ACTIVITIES & REMINDERS

DATE:

Today's Message:
_____
_____

SCRIPTURE _____

## SERMON Notes:

_____
_____
_____
_____
_____
_____
_____
_____
_____
_____
_____
_____
_____
_____
_____
_____
_____
_____
_____
_____
_____
_____
_____
_____
_____
_____
_____

# How Does This Message Challenge Me?

_____
_____
_____
_____
_____
_____
_____
_____

## HOW CAN I APPLY THE LESSON THIS WEEK?

## Prayer Requests

_____
_____
_____
_____
_____
_____
_____
_____

## UPCOMING ACTIVITIES & REMINDERS

DATE:

Today's Message:

_____

_____

# SCRIPTURE

SERMON *Notes:*

# How Does This Message Challenge Me?

_____
_____
_____
_____
_____
_____
_____
_____

## HOW CAN I APPLY THE LESSON THIS WEEK?

## Prayer Requests

_____
_____
_____
_____
_____
_____
_____
_____
_____
_____

## UPCOMING ACTIVITIES & REMINDERS

DATE:

Today's Message:

_____

_____

SCRIPTURE ___

SERMON Notes:

# How Does This Message Challenge Me?

_____
_____
_____
_____
_____
_____

## HOW CAN I APPLY THE LESSON THIS WEEK?

## Prayer Requests

_____
_____
_____
_____
_____
_____
_____
_____

## UPCOMING ACTIVITIES & REMINDERS

DATE:

Today's Message:
_____
_____

SCRIPTURE

SERMON Notes:

# How Does This Message Challenge Me?

_____
_____
_____
_____
_____
_____
_____
_____

## HOW CAN I APPLY THE LESSON THIS WEEK?

## Prayer Requests

_____
_____
_____
_____
_____
_____
_____
_____

## UPCOMING ACTIVITIES & REMINDERS

DATE:

Today's Message:

_____

_____

SCRIPTURE

SERMON Notes:

# How Does This Message Challenge Me?

_____
_____
_____
_____
_____
_____
_____

## HOW CAN I APPLY THE LESSON THIS WEEK?

## Prayer Requests

_____
_____
_____
_____
_____
_____
_____
_____
_____

## UPCOMING ACTIVITIES & REMINDERS

DATE:

Today's Message:

_____

_____

SCRIPTURE

SERMON Notes:

# How Does This Message Challenge Me?

_____
_____
_____
_____
_____
_____
_____

## HOW CAN I APPLY THE LESSON THIS WEEK?

## Prayer Requests

_____
_____
_____
_____
_____
_____
_____
_____

## UPCOMING ACTIVITIES & REMINDERS

DATE:

Today's Message:
_____
_____

SCRIPTURE

SERMON Notes:

_____
_____
_____
_____
_____
_____
_____
_____
_____
_____
_____
_____
_____
_____
_____
_____
_____
_____
_____
_____
_____
_____
_____
_____
_____
_____
_____
_____
_____
_____
_____
_____

# How Does This Message Challenge Me?

_____
_____
_____
_____
_____
_____
_____

## HOW CAN I APPLY THE LESSON THIS WEEK?




## Prayer Requests

_____
_____
_____
_____
_____
_____
_____
_____

## UPCOMING ACTIVITIES & REMINDERS

DATE:

Today's Message:
_____
_____

SCRIPTURE ——

SERMON Notes:

# How Does This Message Challenge Me?

_____
_____
_____
_____
_____
_____
_____

## HOW CAN I APPLY THE LESSON THIS WEEK?

## Prayer Requests

_____
_____
_____
_____
_____
_____
_____
_____

## UPCOMING ACTIVITIES & REMINDERS

DATE:

Today's Message:

SCRIPTURE

SERMON Notes:

# How Does This Message Challenge Me?

_____
_____
_____
_____
_____
_____
_____

## HOW CAN I APPLY THE LESSON THIS WEEK?

## Prayer Requests

_____
_____
_____
_____
_____
_____
_____
_____

## UPCOMING ACTIVITIES & REMINDERS

DATE:

Today's Message:

_____

_____

SCRIPTURE

SERMON Notes:

# How Does This Message Challenge Me?

_____
_____
_____
_____
_____
_____
_____

## HOW CAN I APPLY THE LESSON THIS WEEK?




## Prayer Requests

_____
_____
_____
_____
_____
_____
_____
_____

## UPCOMING ACTIVITIES & REMINDERS

DATE:

Today's Message:

_____

_____

SCRIPTURE

SERMON Notes:

# How Does This Message Challenge Me?

_____
_____
_____
_____
_____
_____

## HOW CAN I APPLY THE LESSON THIS WEEK?




## Prayer Requests

_____
_____
_____
_____
_____
_____
_____
_____

## UPCOMING ACTIVITIES & REMINDERS

**DATE:**

*Today's Message:*

_____

_____

# SCRIPTURE

SERMON *Notes:*

_____
_____
_____
_____
_____
_____
_____
_____
_____
_____
_____
_____
_____
_____
_____
_____
_____
_____
_____
_____
_____
_____
_____
_____
_____
_____
_____
_____

# How Does This Message Challenge Me?

_____
_____
_____
_____
_____
_____
_____

### HOW CAN I APPLY THE LESSON THIS WEEK?

## Prayer Requests

_____
_____
_____
_____
_____
_____
_____
_____

### UPCOMING ACTIVITIES & REMINDERS

DATE:

## Today's Message:

_____

_____

# SCRIPTURE

## SERMON Notes:

_____
_____
_____
_____
_____
_____
_____
_____
_____
_____
_____
_____
_____
_____
_____
_____
_____
_____
_____
_____
_____
_____
_____
_____
_____
_____
_____
_____
_____
_____
_____
_____
_____
_____
_____
_____

# How Does This Message Challenge Me?

_____
_____
_____
_____
_____
_____
_____

## HOW CAN I APPLY THE LESSON THIS WEEK?

## Prayer Requests

_____
_____
_____
_____
_____
_____
_____
_____
_____

## UPCOMING ACTIVITIES & REMINDERS

DATE:

Today's Message:

_____

_____

# SCRIPTURE

SERMON *Notes:*

# How Does This Message Challenge Me?

_____
_____
_____
_____
_____
_____
_____

## HOW CAN I APPLY THE LESSON THIS WEEK?

## Prayer Requests

_____
_____
_____
_____
_____
_____
_____
_____

## UPCOMING ACTIVITIES & REMINDERS

DATE:

Today's Message:
_____
_____

SCRIPTURE _____

SERMON Notes:

# How Does This Message Challenge Me?

_____
_____
_____
_____
_____
_____
_____

## HOW CAN I APPLY THE LESSON THIS WEEK?




## Prayer Requests

_____
_____
_____
_____
_____
_____
_____
_____
_____

## UPCOMING ACTIVITIES & REMINDERS

DATE:

Today's Message:
_____
_____

SCRIPTURE _____

SERMON Notes:

_____
_____
_____
_____
_____
_____
_____
_____
_____
_____
_____
_____
_____
_____
_____
_____
_____
_____
_____
_____
_____
_____
_____
_____
_____
_____
_____
_____

# How Does This Message Challenge Me?

_____
_____
_____
_____
_____
_____
_____

## HOW CAN I APPLY THE LESSON THIS WEEK?

## Prayer Requests

_____
_____
_____
_____
_____
_____
_____
_____

## UPCOMING ACTIVITIES & REMINDERS

DATE:

Today's Message:

_____

_____

SCRIPTURE

SERMON Notes:

# How Does This Message Challenge Me?

_____
_____
_____
_____
_____
_____
_____

## HOW CAN I APPLY THE LESSON THIS WEEK?

## Prayer Requests

_____
_____
_____
_____
_____
_____
_____
_____
_____

## UPCOMING ACTIVITIES & REMINDERS

DATE:

*Today's Message:*

_____

_____

## SCRIPTURE

## SERMON *Notes:*

# How Does This Message Challenge Me?

_____
_____
_____
_____
_____
_____
_____
_____

## HOW CAN I APPLY THE LESSON THIS WEEK?




## Prayer Requests

_____
_____
_____
_____
_____
_____
_____
_____
_____

## UPCOMING ACTIVITIES & REMINDERS

DATE:

Today's Message:
_____
_____

SCRIPTURE _____

SERMON Notes:

# How Does This Message Challenge Me?

HOW CAN I APPLY THE LESSON THIS WEEK?

## Prayer Requests

UPCOMING ACTIVITIES & REMINDERS

DATE:

Today's Message:

_____

_____

SCRIPTURE

SERMON Notes:

# How Does This Message Challenge Me?

_____
_____
_____
_____
_____
_____
_____

## HOW CAN I APPLY THE LESSON THIS WEEK?




## Prayer Requests

_____
_____
_____
_____
_____
_____
_____
_____
_____

## UPCOMING ACTIVITIES & REMINDERS

DATE:

Today's Message:
_____
_____

SCRIPTURE ——

SERMON Notes:

_____
_____
_____
_____
_____
_____
_____
_____
_____
_____
_____
_____
_____
_____
_____
_____
_____
_____
_____
_____
_____
_____
_____
_____

# How Does This Message Challenge Me?

_____
_____
_____
_____
_____
_____
_____

## HOW CAN I APPLY THE LESSON THIS WEEK?

## Prayer Requests

_____
_____
_____
_____
_____
_____
_____
_____

## UPCOMING ACTIVITIES & REMINDERS

DATE:

Today's Message:
_____

_____

SCRIPTURE

SERMON Notes:

# How Does This Message Challenge Me?

_____
_____
_____
_____
_____
_____
_____

## HOW CAN I APPLY THE LESSON THIS WEEK?

## Prayer Requests

_____
_____
_____
_____
_____
_____
_____
_____
_____

## UPCOMING ACTIVITIES & REMINDERS

DATE:

Today's Message:

_____

_____

SCRIPTURE

SERMON Notes:

_____
_____
_____
_____
_____
_____
_____
_____
_____
_____
_____
_____
_____
_____
_____
_____
_____
_____
_____
_____
_____
_____
_____
_____
_____
_____
_____
_____
_____
_____

# How Does This Message Challenge Me?

_____
_____
_____
_____
_____
_____
_____
_____

## HOW CAN I APPLY THE LESSON THIS WEEK?




## Prayer Requests

_____
_____
_____
_____
_____
_____
_____
_____
_____

## UPCOMING ACTIVITIES & REMINDERS

DATE:

Today's Message:
_____

_____

SCRIPTURE

SERMON *Notes:*

# How Does This Message Challenge Me?

_____
_____
_____
_____
_____
_____
_____

## HOW CAN I APPLY THE LESSON THIS WEEK?




## Prayer Requests

_____
_____
_____
_____
_____
_____
_____
_____
_____

## UPCOMING ACTIVITIES & REMINDERS

DATE:

Today's Message:

_____

_____

SCRIPTURE

SERMON Notes:

_____
_____
_____
_____
_____
_____
_____
_____
_____
_____
_____
_____
_____
_____
_____
_____
_____
_____
_____
_____
_____
_____
_____
_____
_____
_____
_____

# How Does This Message Challenge Me?

_____
_____
_____
_____
_____
_____

## HOW CAN I APPLY THE LESSON THIS WEEK?

## Prayer Requests

_____
_____
_____
_____
_____
_____
_____

## UPCOMING ACTIVITIES & REMINDERS

DATE:

*Today's Message:*

_____

_____

## SCRIPTURE

SERMON *Notes:*

_____
_____
_____
_____
_____
_____
_____
_____
_____
_____
_____
_____
_____
_____
_____
_____
_____
_____
_____
_____
_____
_____
_____
_____
_____
_____
_____
_____
_____

# How Does This Message Challenge Me?

_____
_____
_____
_____
_____
_____
_____

## HOW CAN I APPLY THE LESSON THIS WEEK?




## Prayer Requests

_____
_____
_____
_____
_____
_____
_____
_____
_____

## UPCOMING ACTIVITIES & REMINDERS

DATE:

Today's Message:

_____

_____

## SCRIPTURE

## SERMON Notes:

# How Does This Message Challenge Me?

_____
_____
_____
_____
_____
_____

## HOW CAN I APPLY THE LESSON THIS WEEK?

## Prayer Requests

_____
_____
_____
_____
_____
_____
_____

## UPCOMING ACTIVITIES & REMINDERS

DATE:

Today's Message:
_____
_____

SCRIPTURE

SERMON Notes:

# How Does This Message Challenge Me?

_____
_____
_____
_____
_____
_____
_____

## HOW CAN I APPLY THE LESSON THIS WEEK?

## Prayer Requests

_____
_____
_____
_____
_____
_____
_____
_____
_____

## UPCOMING ACTIVITIES & REMINDERS

DATE:

Today's Message:
_____
_____

SCRIPTURE

SERMON Notes:

_____
_____
_____
_____
_____
_____
_____
_____
_____
_____
_____
_____
_____
_____
_____
_____
_____
_____
_____
_____
_____
_____
_____
_____
_____
_____
_____

# How Does This Message Challenge Me?

_____
_____
_____
_____
_____
_____
_____

## HOW CAN I APPLY THE LESSON THIS WEEK?

## Prayer Requests

_____
_____
_____
_____
_____
_____
_____
_____

## UPCOMING ACTIVITIES & REMINDERS

DATE:

Today's Message:

_____

_____

SCRIPTURE

SERMON Notes:

_____
_____
_____
_____
_____
_____
_____
_____
_____
_____
_____
_____
_____
_____
_____
_____
_____
_____
_____
_____
_____
_____
_____
_____
_____

# How Does This Message Challenge Me?

_____
_____
_____
_____
_____
_____
_____

## HOW CAN I APPLY THE LESSON THIS WEEK?

## Prayer Requests

_____
_____
_____
_____
_____
_____
_____
_____

## UPCOMING ACTIVITIES & REMINDERS

DATE:

*Today's Message:*

_____

_____

# SCRIPTURE

## SERMON *Notes:*

_____
_____
_____
_____
_____
_____
_____
_____
_____
_____
_____
_____
_____
_____
_____
_____
_____
_____
_____
_____
_____
_____
_____
_____
_____
_____
_____
_____
_____
_____
_____

# How Does This Message Challenge Me?

_____
_____
_____
_____
_____
_____
_____

## HOW CAN I APPLY THE LESSON THIS WEEK?




## Prayer Requests

_____
_____
_____
_____
_____
_____
_____
_____
_____

## UPCOMING ACTIVITIES & REMINDERS

DATE:

Today's Message:

_____

_____

SCRIPTURE

SERMON Notes:

_____
_____
_____
_____
_____
_____
_____
_____
_____
_____
_____
_____
_____
_____
_____
_____
_____
_____
_____
_____
_____
_____
_____
_____
_____
_____
_____

# How Does This Message Challenge Me?

_____
_____
_____
_____
_____
_____
_____
_____

## HOW CAN I APPLY THE LESSON THIS WEEK?




## Prayer Requests

_____
_____
_____
_____
_____
_____
_____
_____
_____
_____

## UPCOMING ACTIVITIES & REMINDERS

DATE:

*Today's Message:*

_____

_____

# SCRIPTURE

SERMON *Notes:*

# How Does This Message Challenge Me?

_____
_____
_____
_____
_____
_____

## HOW CAN I APPLY THE LESSON THIS WEEK?

## Prayer Requests

_____
_____
_____
_____
_____
_____
_____
_____

## UPCOMING ACTIVITIES & REMINDERS

DATE:

Today's Message:

_____

_____

SCRIPTURE ——————

SERMON Notes:

# How Does This Message Challenge Me?

_____
_____
_____
_____
_____
_____
_____
_____

## HOW CAN I APPLY THE LESSON THIS WEEK?

## Prayer Requests

_____
_____
_____
_____
_____
_____
_____
_____
_____

## UPCOMING ACTIVITIES & REMINDERS

DATE:

Today's Message:
_____
_____

SCRIPTURE

SERMON *Notes:*

_____
_____
_____
_____
_____
_____
_____
_____
_____
_____
_____
_____
_____
_____
_____
_____
_____
_____
_____
_____
_____
_____
_____
_____
_____
_____
_____
_____

# How Does This Message Challenge Me?

_____

_____

_____

_____

_____

_____

_____

## HOW CAN I APPLY THE LESSON THIS WEEK?

## Prayer Requests

_____

_____

_____

_____

_____

_____

_____

_____

_____

## UPCOMING ACTIVITIES & REMINDERS

DATE:

Today's Message:

_____

_____

SCRIPTURE

SERMON Notes:

_____
_____
_____
_____
_____
_____
_____
_____
_____
_____
_____
_____
_____
_____
_____
_____
_____
_____
_____
_____
_____
_____
_____
_____
_____
_____
_____

# How Does This Message Challenge Me?

_____
_____
_____
_____
_____
_____
_____

## HOW CAN I APPLY THE LESSON THIS WEEK?




## Prayer Requests

_____
_____
_____
_____
_____
_____
_____
_____

## UPCOMING ACTIVITIES & REMINDERS

DATE:

Today's Message:

_____

_____

SCRIPTURE _____

SERMON Notes:

# How Does This Message Challenge Me?

_____
_____
_____
_____
_____
_____
_____

## HOW CAN I APPLY THE LESSON THIS WEEK?

## Prayer Requests

_____
_____
_____
_____
_____
_____
_____
_____

## UPCOMING ACTIVITIES & REMINDERS

DATE:

Today's Message:

_____

_____

SCRIPTURE ——

SERMON Notes:

_____
_____
_____
_____
_____
_____
_____
_____
_____
_____
_____
_____
_____
_____
_____
_____
_____
_____
_____
_____
_____
_____
_____
_____
_____

# How Does This Message Challenge Me?

_____
_____
_____
_____
_____
_____
_____
_____

## HOW CAN I APPLY THE LESSON THIS WEEK?




## Prayer Requests

_____
_____
_____
_____
_____
_____
_____
_____

## UPCOMING ACTIVITIES & REMINDERS

DATE:

Today's Message:
_____

_____

SCRIPTURE _____

SERMON Notes:

_____
_____
_____
_____
_____
_____
_____
_____
_____
_____
_____
_____
_____
_____
_____
_____
_____
_____
_____
_____
_____
_____
_____
_____
_____
_____
_____
_____
_____
_____
_____
_____

# How Does This Message Challenge Me?

_____
_____
_____
_____
_____
_____

## HOW CAN I APPLY THE LESSON THIS WEEK?




## Prayer Requests

_____
_____
_____
_____
_____
_____
_____
_____
_____

## UPCOMING ACTIVITIES & REMINDERS

DATE:

Today's Message:

_____

_____

SCRIPTURE

SERMON Notes:

# How Does This Message Challenge Me?

_____
_____
_____
_____
_____
_____
_____

## HOW CAN I APPLY THE LESSON THIS WEEK?

## Prayer Requests

_____
_____
_____
_____
_____
_____
_____
_____

## UPCOMING ACTIVITIES & REMINDERS

DATE:

*Today's Message:*

_____

_____

# SCRIPTURE ___

SERMON *Notes:*

# How Does This Message Challenge Me?

_____
_____
_____
_____
_____
_____
_____

## HOW CAN I APPLY THE LESSON THIS WEEK?

## Prayer Requests

_____
_____
_____
_____
_____
_____
_____
_____
_____

## UPCOMING ACTIVITIES & REMINDERS

DATE:

Today's Message:

_____

_____

SCRIPTURE

SERMON Notes:

_____
_____
_____
_____
_____
_____
_____
_____
_____
_____
_____
_____
_____
_____
_____
_____
_____
_____
_____
_____
_____
_____
_____
_____
_____
_____
_____
_____

# How Does This Message Challenge Me?

_____
_____
_____
_____
_____
_____
_____

## HOW CAN I APPLY THE LESSON THIS WEEK?

## Prayer Requests

_____
_____
_____
_____
_____
_____
_____
_____
_____

## UPCOMING ACTIVITIES & REMINDERS

# THOUGHTS & IDEAS

# THOUGHTS & IDEAS

# THOUGHTS & IDEAS

# THOUGHTS & IDEAS

# THOUGHTS & IDEAS

# THOUGHTS & IDEAS

# THOUGHTS & IDEAS